Nebraska

BY ANN HEINRICHS

Content Adviser: Mary Jackson, Coordinator of Children's and Young Adult Service, Nebraska Library Commission, Lincoln, Nebraska

Reading Adviser: Dr. Linda D. Labbo, Department of Reading Education, College of Education, The University of Georgia

COMPASS POINT BOOKS ✦ MINNEAPOLIS, MINNESOTA

Compass Point Books
3109 West 50th Street, #115
Minneapolis, MN 55410

Visit Compass Point Books on the Internet at *www.compasspointbooks.com*
or e-mail your request to *custserv@compasspointbooks.com*

On the cover: Scotts Bluff National Monument

Photographs ©: Steve Mulligan, cover, 1; James P. Rowan, 3, 5, 34, 36, 41, 48 (top); John Elk III, 7, 33, 38, 39, 43 (top), 45, 47; Unicorn Stock Photos/Jim Shippee, 8, 9, 18, 42; Photo Network/Bill Terry, 10; Unicorn Stock Photos/Paula J. Harrington, 11, 21; Stock Montage, Inc., 12, 32 (bottom); North Wind Picture Archives, 13, 14, 16; Hulton/Archive by Getty Images, 15, 17, 30, 32 (top), 46; Unicorn Stock Photos/Chuck Schmeiser, 19; Getty Images/Alex Wong, 22; Unicorn Stock Photos/Joel Dexter, 23; Unicorn Stock Photos/Mark Romesser, 24; Corbis/Vince Streano, 26; PhotoDisc, 27, 44 (bottom); Michael C. Snell, 28; Index Stock Imagery/Henry Horenstein, 29; Cheryl Richter, 31; Unicorn Stock Photos/Jean Higgins, 37; Getty Images/Eric Francis, 40; Robesus, Inc., 43 (state flag); One Mile Up, Inc., 43 (state seal); Robert McCaw, 44 (top and middle).

Editors: E. Russell Primm, Emily J. Dolbear, and Christianne C. Jones
Photo Researcher: Marcie C. Spence
Photo Selector: Linda S. Koutris
Designer: The Design Lab
Cartographer: XNR Productions, Inc.

Library of Congress Cataloging-in-Publication Data
Heinrichs, Ann.
  Nebraska / by Ann Heinrichs.
      p. cm. — (This land is your land)
 Summary: Introduces the geography, history, government, people, culture, and attractions of Nebraska. Includes bibliographical references and index.
  ISBN 0-7565-0356-6 (alk. paper)
  1. Nebraska—Juvenile literature. [1. Nebraska.] I. Title. II. Series.
  F666.3.H45 2004
  978.2—dc21   2003005408

Table of Contents

NOTE: In this book, words that are defined in the glossary are in **bold** the first time they appear in the text.

Mattie Oblinger was a **pioneer** on the Nebraska **prairie.** She wrote to friends in 1873: "I suppose you would like to see us in our sod house," she said. "I ripped our wagon sheet in two [and] have it around two sides. . . . The only objection I have [is] we have no floor yet."

Like many Nebraska pioneers, Mattie lived in a sod house. Sod is the top layer of soil with the attached grass and roots. You could say the pioneers built their state from the ground up!

Many pioneers arrived along the Oregon Trail. They braved snowstorms, dust storms, and grasshopper **swarms.** In time, Nebraska became one of America's top farming states.

Nebraska is a leader in corn, beef cattle, and many other farm products. Grassy prairies and fertile plains cover almost the whole state. Nebraska's factories make food products, chemicals, and machines. The state is also a center for the insurance and telemarketing **industries.**

Nebraska is rich in history. Tourists explore its **prehistoric** sites, pioneer villages, and much more. Now come along and explore Nebraska yourself!

▲ **Nebraska prairie**

Nebraska is one of America's midwestern states. It has six other states as neighbors. To the north is South Dakota. To the east are Iowa and a little bit of Missouri. Kansas lies to the south, and Wyoming is to the west. A big, square notch cuts into Nebraska's southwest corner. Part of Colorado fits into that notch.

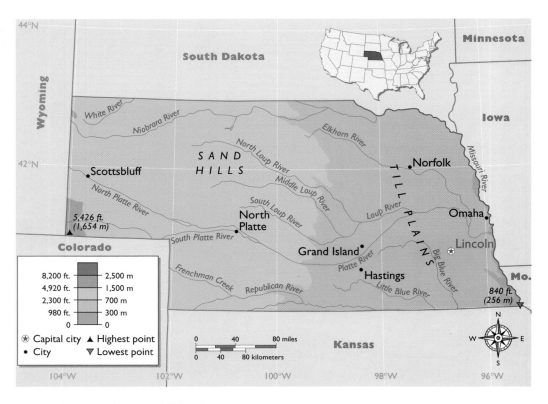

▲ **A topographic map of Nebraska**

▲ **The Platte River flows past Grand Island.**

Nebraska's rivers were "highways" for early settlers. The Missouri River forms Nebraska's entire eastern border. It curves around to create part of its northern border, too. The Missouri is a major tributary, or branch, of the great Mississippi River.

The Platte River is formed where the North Platte and South Platte Rivers meet. It then flows into the Missouri. The Oto Indians called the Platte River *Nebraska,* meaning "flat water." That's how Nebraska got its name.

Rolling prairies cover much of the state. Huge glaciers, or sheets of ice, once moved across eastern Nebraska. They left behind till, which is clay, sand, and gravel. This area is called the Till Plains. It's one of Nebraska's richest farming regions.

Central and western Nebraska lie in the nation's Great Plains. The dry Sand Hills region is in north-central Nebraska. Many cattle ranches are located there. The cattle graze on grasses growing in the sandy soil.

▲ The grassy hills of the Sand Hills region

▲ A buffalo cow and calf at the Fort Niobrara National Wildlife Refuge

Tall prairie grasses still wave across the rolling plains. One is little bluestem, the state grass. Great herds of bison, or buffalo, once roamed Nebraska's grasslands. Today, a small buffalo herd lives in the Fort Niobrara National Wildlife Refuge.

Nebraska has little forestland. The Nebraska National Forest is like an island amid the Sand Hills. In the 1800s, people planted thousands of pine trees there. These trees shelter mule deer, white-tailed deer, and wild turkeys. Coyotes, prairie dogs, and jackrabbits also live in Nebraska.

Every March, thousands of long-legged sandhill cranes begin flying into Nebraska. Birdwatchers head for the Platte River to watched the cranes "dance." The cranes strut and hop around with outspread wings.

Nebraska gets hot summers and cold winters. Tornadoes often strike in the

▲ **Prairie dogs live in Nebraska.**

summer. In the winter, blizzards sweep across the prairie. Their fierce winds and blinding snow can make travel impossible. Southeastern Nebraska gets the most rain and snow. The west, however, is dry.

▲ **Snow surrounds a red barn near Ponca.**

Many Native Americans once made their homes in Nebraska. The area was a hunting ground for several tribes. They moved from place to place following great buffalo herds. Among these people were the Brulé, Oglala Sioux (Dakota), Arapaho, Comanche, and Cheyenne. The Pawnee often clashed with other tribes. They were both buffalo hunters and farmers.

Some groups settled in villages in eastern and central Nebraska. They included the Ponca, Omaha, and Oto. They lived by fishing, hunting, and farming.

▲ **An Omaha Indian hunting with a bow and arrow**

French explorers were the first Europeans in Nebraska. René-Robert Cavelier, Sieur de La Salle, never set foot in the region. However, in 1682, he claimed the Mississippi River Valley for France. This included present-day Nebraska. La Salle named this vast region Louisiana, after King Louis XIV of France. The French fur traders Pierre and Paul Mallet arrived in 1739. They were probably the first non-Native Americans to cross Nebraska.

▲ La Salle claiming the Mississippi River Valley for France in 1682

The United States purchased Louisiana Territory in 1803. Meriwether Lewis and William Clark were sent to explore this new land. As they traveled up the Missouri River, they explored eastern Nebraska. Zebulon Pike passed through in 1806. In 1820, an engineer named Stephen H. Long explored the area. He called Nebraska's treeless plains the Great American Desert, which discouraged settlers from coming to Nebraska for a long time.

At first, settlers only passed through Nebraska. Pioneers began crossing Nebraska on the Oregon Trail in 1843. They

▲ **Lewis and Clark met Native Americans during their exploration of Louisiana Territory.**

▲ This family of settlers stopped in Loup Valley in 1886 as they traveled to their new homestead.

looked forward to farming, trapping, and mining farther west. In 1854, Congress passed the Kansas-Nebraska Act. It established both Kansas Territory and Nebraska Territory.

By then, word had spread that Nebraska wasn't such a desert after all. Waves of new settlers poured in. They grew wheat, barley, oats, and corn on the fertile plains. The cattle grazed on the rolling grasslands.

The **Homestead** Act of 1862 granted free land to settlers. That attracted even more newcomers. In 1867, Nebraska became the thirty-seventh U.S. state. At that time, it was home to about 120,000 people.

Nebraska's farmers struggled to survive. With few trees for wood, many settlers built sod houses. Grasshoppers swarmed through the western states in the 1870s. They destroyed Nebraska's crops. Drought, or lack of rain, was another problem.

Irrigation projects often helped the farmers. They channeled water from rivers to faraway fields. The North Platte River Project began in 1905. It brought water to crops in western Nebraska.

From 1934 to 1935, fierce winds blew across America's plains. These dust storms blew away tons of soil. This was another setback for Nebraska's farmers.

▲ **A Nebraska farmer stands in a field of dying crops during a drought.**

▲ **A woman inspects bomb casings at an Omaha factory in 1944.**

Petroleum (oil) was discovered in southeastern Nebraska in 1939. Oil became Nebraska's most valuable mineral. During World War II (1939–1945), Nebraska supplied food for American troops. A huge aircraft plant opened near Omaha in 1940. It later became the headquarters for the Strategic Air Command, now called Strategic Command or Stratcom. This base controls America's long-range **missiles.**

In the 1950s, big farm companies began buying farmland. As a result, many small family farms closed. State leaders began to see that Nebraska relied too heavily on farming. They tried to attract new industries to the state. Soon, new factories were making food products, chemicals, and machinery.

In 1982, Nebraska passed Initiative 300. This act says that individual farmers cannot sell their farms and ranches to companies. Nebraskans are still divided over Initiative 300. Some say it protects family farms. Others say it slows down development. Initiative 300 will continue to be an important issue in the years to come.

▲ **An American flag painted on a barn on a Nebraska farm**

Do you know who makes your state laws? Members of your state legislature do. Do you know how your state legislature is designed? Well, it probably has two chambers, or houses. In most states, those two houses are the senate and the house of representatives.

Nebraska works differently, though. Nebraska is the only state with a unicameral legislature. That means it has only one house. Nebraska's forty-nine state lawmakers are all called senators. They meet in the state's "skyscraper" capitol in Lincoln.

In other ways, Nebraska's government is like other state

▲ The state capitol in Lincoln

governments. It's similar to the U.S. government, too. Like the U.S. government, the governing power is divided into three branches—legislative, executive, and judicial. This makes for a good balance of power.

Nebraska's governor is the head of the executive branch. This branch makes sure the state's laws are carried out. Nebraska voters elect a governor every four years. They also elect five important executive officers. The governor and

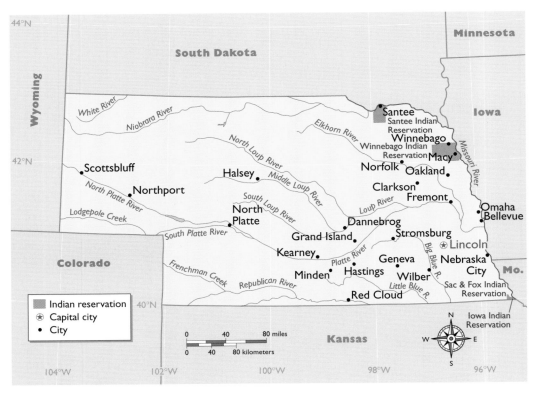

▲ **A geopolitical map of Nebraska**

▲ Judges decide cases in the Sherman County Courthouse in Loup City.

state treasurer may serve only two terms in a row. The other officers may serve any number of terms.

The judicial branch is made up of judges. They listen to cases and consider whether laws have been broken. Nebraska's highest court is the state supreme court. It has seven justices, or judges. The governor appoints new judges in Nebraska's courts. After that, voters decide whether or not those judges may stay.

Nebraska is divided into ninety-three counties. In most counties, voters elect three to five county commissioners. In

▲ **Vice President Richard
Cheney was born in Lincoln.**

others, they elect seven county supervisors. Most Nebraska cities elect a mayor or manager and a city council. Nebraska City is different. It's governed by a board of commissioners. In villages, people usually elect a board of five trustees. If a city has more than five thousand people, it may choose home rule. That means it may draw up its own charter, or basic set of laws. Lincoln and Omaha have chosen to do this.

One Nebraskan tried to be president but never made it. William Jennings Bryan ran for president three times—in 1896, 1900, and 1908. Another person born in Nebraska became president without trying! Gerald Ford was vice president under Richard Nixon. When Nixon resigned in 1974, Ford became the thirty-eighth president. Richard Cheney became vice president under George W. Bush in 2001.

Nebraska is one of America's greatest farming states. It ranks among the top ten states in an amazing number of products. These include beef cattle, corn, sorghum, hay, soybeans, hogs and pigs, sugar beets, and even sunflowers!

Beef cattle cover the most farmland in Nebraska and bring in the most farm income. Hogs are also important. Many farmers produce dairy cattle, chickens, and eggs, as well. Corn is Nebraska's top crop. Soybeans, wheat, sorghum, and hay are valuable crops, too.

▲ Corn is Nebraska's top crop.

▲ Cattle are the largest source of Nebraska's farm income.

What becomes of all these farm products? Much of the corn, hay, and sorghum becomes food for cattle and hogs. Some corn is exported to other countries. It is also made into ethanol, a type of fuel. Corn gave Nebraska its nickname, the Cornhusker State. Husking means removing the corn's leafy outer casing.

Nebraska's major factories include food processing and packaging plants. Many farm products go to food-processing plants. Nebraska is one of the biggest meat-packing centers in the world. Nebraska's wheat is made into cereal and baked goods. Other food plants produce milk, butter, cheese, and soft drinks.

Nebraska has many other factory goods, too. Some factories produce chemicals including medicines, fertilizers, and insect killers. Others make farm equipment such as tractors. Some even turn out scientific and medical instruments and electrical equipment.

Natural resources are valuable to Nebraska. Petroleum (oil) is the state's leading mineral. Most of the oil comes from southeastern Nebraska. Miners dig sand and gravel from the Platte River Valley. These materials are used for building roads and making cement. Clay and limestone are also mined in Nebraska.

Many Nebraskans work in service industries. Did you ever get a phone call from a telemarketer? Telemarketers call people and try to to sell them something. Telemarketing is a

▲ **A worker inspects a model of an oil refinery plant in Omaha.**

big industry in Nebraska. It's one of the state's many service industries. Another service industry is the wholesale trade business. Wholesalers buy goods such as farm products and farm supplies. Then they sell those goods to other businesses. Insurance sales, military service, teaching, and health care are service industries, too.

Most Nebraskans used to live on farms. Today, however, about two out of three Nebraskans live in city areas. In fact, more than half the state's residents live within five eastern counties. These counties surround Omaha and Lincoln.

▲ **Omaha is the largest city in Nebraska.**

Omaha is Nebraska's largest city. The second-largest is Lincoln, the state capital. Next in size are Bellevue, Grand Island, Kearney, and Fremont. Nebraska ranks thirty-eighth in population among all the states. In 2000, it was home to 1,711,263 people.

Nebraskans have roots in many countries. Swedes, Bohemians, and Russians were among Nebraska's early settlers. German, Danish, Irish, and Italian people also settled in Nebraska. Today, about nine out of ten Nebraskans are white.

▲ **The Hall County Courthouse is located in Grand Island.**

▲ **A man walking on stilts at the Nebraska State Fair in Lincoln**

African-Americans, **Hispanics,** Asians, and Native Americans add to Nebraska's **ethnic** mix.

County fairs take place all over the state. The Nebraska State Fair in Lincoln is the biggest fair in the state. Some people show off their prize crops and farm animals. Others check out the latest farm equipment and sample delicious foods.

▲ **William "Buffalo Bill" Cody in 1915**

"Buffalo Bill" Cody settled on a ranch near North Platte in 1879. He began his famous Wild West Show there. The show toured the United States and Europe. Today, North Platte holds Nebraskaland Days and the Buffalo Bill Rodeo every summer.

Nebraska's many ethnic groups host festivals, too. Danish people in Dannebrog celebrate Grundlovs Fest. Both Stromsburg and Oakland hold Swedish festivals. Czech festivals take place in Wilber and Clarkson. Omaha has an Italian festival, and Scottsbluff hosts the Hispanic Cinco de Mayo festival. Native Americans gather in Winnebago for the Winnebago Powwow. Macy holds the Omaha Powwow. The Santee Sioux Powwow is in Santee.

Every year on April 22, people all over the country celebrate Arbor Day. This holiday was founded by Nebraskan J. Sterling Morton in 1872. Arbor Day is a day for planting trees. *Arbor* is the Latin word for tree.

▲ Polka dancing is one of the many activities visitors can see during the Czech festival every August in Wilber.

Famous actor and dancer Fred Astaire in 1934

Author Willa Cather was from Nebraska.

Dozens of actors came from Nebraska. They include superstars Marlon Brando and Henry Fonda. Nick Nolte, James Coburn, and Montgomery Clift all started out in Nebraska. The dancing actor Fred Astaire was also a Nebraskan.

Willa Cather grew up near Red Cloud. She became one of America's greatest writers. She wrote *O Pioneers!* (1913) and other novels. John Neihardt is famous for his lengthy poem *Black Elk Speaks* (1932).

To Nebraskans, football means just one thing—the Cornhuskers! The University of Nebraska's football team is one of the "winningest" teams in college football. By 2002, the Huskers had a stunning record. They had forty winning seasons and thirty-four bowl game appearances in a row. Go Big Red!

To begin, let's go back millions of years in time. Herds of animals drowned near the Niobrara River. Some were tiny camels. Others were gigantic pigs. Their remains were discovered at Agate Fossil Beds. You can still see hoofprints and rock-hard bones there today.

Giant woolly mammoths once thundered across Nebraska. In 1922, scientists in Nebraska discovered the largest woolly mammoth skeleton. They named it Archie.

▲ **Prehistoric skeletons at the Agate Fossil Beds Visitor Center**

Archie's shoulder stood 13 feet (4 meters) high. That's higher than most ceilings! His skeleton is now at the University of Nebraska State Museum in Lincoln. A life-sized Archie statue stands in front of the museum.

While you're in Lincoln, you can visit the "skyscraper" capitol. Lincoln is also home to the Museum of Nebraska History and the Lincoln Children's Museum.

In 1804, Lewis and Clark had just reached Nebraska. They met with Native Americans on a bluff overlooking

▲ Fort Atkinson State Historic Park stands where Lewis and Clark once met with Native Americans.

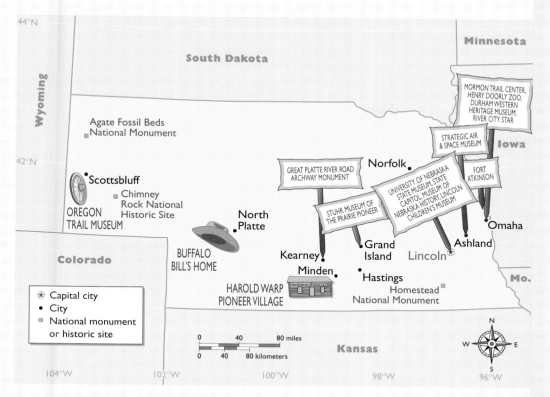

44°N

Minnesota

South Dakota

Wyoming

MORMON TRAIL CENTER,
HENRY DOORLY ZOO,
DURHAM WESTERN
HERITAGE MUSEUM,
RIVER CITY STAR

Agate Fossil Beds
National Monument

STRATEGIC AIR
& SPACE MUSEUM

Iowa

42°N

GREAT PLATTE RIVER ROAD
ARCHWAY MONUMENT

Norfolk

FORT
ATKINSON

Scottsbluff

UNIVERSITY OF NEBRASKA
STATE MUSEUM, STATE
CAPITOL MUSEUM OF
NEBRASKA HISTORY, LINCOLN
CHILDREN'S MUSEUM

Chimney
Rock National
Historic Site

OREGON
TRAIL MUSEUM

STUHR MUSEUM OF
THE PRAIRIE PIONEER

North
Platte

Omaha

Grand
Island

Ashland

BUFFALO
BILL'S HOME

Kearney

Lincoln

Colorado

Minden

Mo.

Hastings

HAROLD WARP
PIONEER VILLAGE

Homestead
National Monument

⊛ Capital city
• City
▪ National monument
  or historic site

0   40   80 miles

0   40   80 kilometers

Kansas

N
W   E
S

104°W   102°W   100°W   98°W   96°W

▲ **Places to visit in Nebraska**

the Missouri River. The site, called Council Bluffs, later
became Fort Atkinson. Today, visitors can see the fort's
workshops and other buildings.

Chimney Rock towers high over the western Nebraska
prairie. Pioneers on the Oregon Trail knew it well. Many
travelers carved their names into the rock. Farther west is
Scotts Bluff. From these colorful cliffs, you can gaze across
the valley below. The site's Oregon Trail Museum explores

▲ Covered wagons sit at the base of Eagle Rock at Scotts Bluff National Monument in Gering.

the region's history. Look around the area, and you'll see wagon-wheel ruts. These are the grooves the pioneers' wagon wheels made in the ground.

Imagine how exciting free land was for a pioneer family. The Homestead Act granted settlers free land. All they had to do was farm the land for five years. Today, the Homestead National Monument stands near Lincoln. Visit an old-fashioned cabin, schoolhouse, and museum at the monument. You'll learn how hard these settlers worked to build their dreams.

Want an inside look at pioneer life? Just visit Stuhr Museum of the Prairie Pioneer in Grand Island. This "museum" spreads across many acres of prairie. You'll see log cabins, a railroad town, and a Pawnee earth lodge. You'll also meet "townspeople"—the blacksmith, tinsmith, marshal, and many others. Sit back, watch them work, and hear their stories.

One of Nebraska's most recent attractions also explores pioneer life. It is the Great Platte River Road Archway

▲ **The Stuhr Museum of the Prairie Pioneer is located in Grand Island.**

Monument, which stretches across Interstate 80 near Kearney. Workers at the monument reenact the journeys and the troubles pioneers faced crossing the state in covered wagons.

How would you like to see Buffalo Bill's Wild West Show? Just visit the barn at Buffalo Bill's home in North Platte. You'll see an actual film of the original show. The film was shot by inventor Thomas Edison.

▲ **The Buffalo Bill Ranch State Historic Site in North Platte**

▲ Visitors examine a plane in the entry hall of the Strategic Air and Space Museum.

The Strategic Air and Space Museum is in Ashland. At the museum, you can visit the past and zoom into the future. Exhibits include historic aircraft and ultramodern jets. You'll also learn what the future holds for air and space travel.

▲ **The Desert Dome, which contains the world's largest indoor desert, is at the Henry Doorly Zoo in Omaha.**

Omaha has many exciting places to visit. Use the touch screens at the Durham Western Heritage Museum. You'll see the past open up before your eyes. Stroll past tigers, elephants, and gorillas at the Henry Doorly Zoo. You can relive pioneer adventures at the Mormon Trail Center. Cruise the Missouri River aboard the River City Star.

Nebraska is a great state to explore. It's a place where the past, present, and future come to life!

Important Dates

1682   René-Robert Cavelier, Sieur de La Salle, claims the Mississippi River Valley for France; this region includes present-day Nebraska.

1714   French explorer Etienne Veniard de Bourgmont travels the Missouri River to the mouth of the Platte River.

1739   Pierre and Paul Mallet are probably the first non-Native Americans to cross Nebraska.

1803   The United States purchases Louisiana Territory, which includes Nebraska.

1804   Meriwether Lewis and William Clark explore eastern Nebraska.

1806   Zebulon Pike crosses south-central Nebraska.

1819   U.S. Army troops set up Fort Atkinson.

1843   Pioneers begin crossing Nebraska on the Oregon Trail.

1854   The Kansas-Nebraska Act establishes Nebraska Territory.

1867   Nebraska becomes the thirty-seventh U.S. state on March 1.

1870s   Grasshoppers damage Nebraska's crops.

1877   Sioux chief Crazy Horse surrenders to the U.S. Army at Fort Robinson.

1905   The North Platte River Project begins; it will irrigate crops in western Nebraska.

1937   Nebraska's unicameral legislature meets for the first time.

1939   Petroleum is discovered in southeastern Nebraska.

1967   Nebraskans celebrate the centennial, or 100th anniversary, of statehood.

1982   Initiative 300 bars farmers from selling their farms or ranches in Nebraska to companies.

1986   Nebraska's governor's race becomes the first in the nation to include two female opponents.

1997   University of Nebraska Cornhuskers are national football champions for the fifth time.

Glossary

ethnic—relating to a culture or nationality

Hispanics—people of Mexican, South American, and other Spanish-speaking cultures

homestead—a piece of land with room for a new home and farm

industries—businesses or trades

missiles—weapons made to be launched through the air toward a target

pioneer—someone who explores or settles in a new land

prairie—flat or rolling grassland

prehistoric—occurring before people began recording history

swarms—large, moving masses or crowds

Did You Know?

★ The world's largest hand-planted forest is in the Nebraska National Forest near Halsey. Its ponderosa pine trees cover about 25,000 acres (10,117 hectares) of land.

★ The first race for governor to include two female opponents took place in Nebraska in 1986. State treasurer Kay Orr defeated Lincoln mayor Helen Boosalis.

★ The 911 emergency system was developed and first used in Lincoln.

★ Nebraska has more miles of river than any other state.

★ In 1921, Father Edward Flanagan founded Boys Town just outside of Omaha for homeless and troubled boys. Flanagan believed there's "no such thing as a bad boy." The home is now Boys and Girls Town. It has grown into a small city within Omaha.

★ Nebraska is one of only four states with a "skyscraper" capitol. The others are Louisiana, North Dakota, and Florida.

At a Glance

State capital: Lincoln

State motto: Equality Before the Law

State nickname: Cornhusker State

Statehood: March 1, 1867; thirty-seventh state

Land area: 75,898 square miles (196,576 sq km); **rank:** fifteenth

Highest point: In southwestern Kimball County, 5,426 feet (1,655 m) above sea level

Lowest point: In Richardson County, 840 feet (256 m) above sea level

Highest recorded temperature: 118°F (48°C) at Minden on July 24, 1936; Hartington on July 17, 1936; and Geneva on July 15, 1934

Lowest recorded temperature: −47°F (−44°C) at Camp Clarke near Northport on February 12, 1899, and Oshkosh on December 22, 1898

Average January temperature: 23°F (−5°C)

Average July temperature: 76°F (24°C)

Population in 2000: 1,711,263; **rank:** thirty-eighth

Largest cities in 2000: Omaha (390,007), Lincoln (225,581), Bellevue (44,382), Grand Island (42,940)

Factory products: Food products, chemicals, machinery

Farm products: Beef cattle, corn, hogs, soybeans

Mining products: Petroleum, sand, gravel

State flag: Nebraska's state flag shows the state seal against a field of blue.

State seal: The state seal shows many symbols of Nebraska's history, nature, and industry. In the background are the Rocky Mountains. Railroad cars are heading toward the mountains. Alongside them, a steamboat ascends the Missouri River. The steamboat and railroad aided the settlement of Nebraska. In the foreground is a blacksmith with his hammer and anvil. He represents the mechanical arts. A settler's cabin and stalks of wheat and corn stand for Nebraska's agriculture. Above the scene is a banner with the state motto, "Equality Before the Law." At the bottom is the date of statehood, March 1st, 1867.

State abbreviations: Nebr. (traditional); NE (postal)

State Symbols

State bird: Western meadowlark

State flower: Goldenrod

State tree: Eastern cottonwood

State mammal: White-tailed deer

State fish: Channel catfish

State insect: Honeybee

State grass: Little bluestem

State rock: Prairie agate

State gem: Blue chalcedony

State fossil: Mammoth

State soil: Holdrege series

State river: Platte River

State beverage: Milk

State soft drink: Kool-Aid

State American folk dance: Square dance

Making Beef and Vegetable Stir-Fry

Nebraska's homegrown farm products make a great stir-fry!

Makes six servings.

INGREDIENTS:

1 1/4 pound beef sirloin

4 cups of your favorite vegetables (broccoli, peppers, shredded carrots, pea pods, etc.)

3 tablespoons water

1 clove garlic, minced

1/2 cup stir-fry sauce

1/4 teaspoon crushed red pepper

3 cups cooked rice

DIRECTIONS:

Make sure an adult helps you with the cutting and the hot stove. Cut the beef in long strips. Then cut the strips into half-inch pieces. Mix the vegetables and water in a large skillet. Cover and cook over medium heat until tender but still crisp (about 4 minutes). Remove vegetables from the skillet and drain the liquid out. Put the beef and garlic in the skillet. Stir-fry until the beef is no longer pink (about 3 to 4 minutes). Add the vegetables, stir-fry sauce, and red pepper. Heat and stir until it's heated through. Serve over rice.

"Beautiful Nebraska"

Words by Jim Fras and Guy G. Miller
Music by Jim Fras

Beautiful Nebraska, peaceful prairieland,
Laced with many rivers, and the hills of sand;
Dark green valleys cradled in the earth,
Rain and sunshine bring abundant birth.
Beautiful Nebraska, as you look around,
You will find a rainbow reaching to the ground;
All these wonders by the Master's hand;
Beautiful Nebraska land.
We are so proud of this state where we live,
There is no place that has so much to give.

Beautiful Nebraska, as you look around,
You will find a rainbow reaching to the ground;
All these wonders by the Master's hand,
Beautiful Nebraska land.

Grover Cleveland Alexander (1887–1950) was one of the greatest pitchers in baseball history. He played with the Philadelphia Phillies and the Chicago Cubs. Alexander was born in Elba.

Fred Astaire (1899–1987) was an actor known for his graceful ballroom dancing. Ginger Rogers often played his partner in movies. Astaire (pictured above left) was born Frederick Austerlitz in Omaha.

Marlon Brando (1924–) is an actor known for his fiery and moody roles. His movies include *Mutiny on the Bounty* (1962) and *The Godfather* (1972). Brando was born in Omaha.

Johnny Carson (1925–) is a comedian who hosted a late night talk show called the *Tonight Show* from 1962 to 1992. He was born in Iowa but grew up in Norfolk.

Willa Cather (1875–1947) was an author who wrote *O Pioneers!* (1913) and many other novels. She was born in Virginia and grew up in Red Cloud.

Montgomery Clift (1920–1966) was an actor. His movies include *A Place in the Sun* (1951) and *Judgment at Nuremberg* (1961). Clift was born in Omaha.

James Coburn (1928–2002) was an actor in many action movies. They include *The Magnificent Seven* (1960) and *The Great Escape* (1963). Coburn was born in Laurel.

Henry Fonda (1905–1982) was an actor. His many movies include *The Grapes of Wrath* (1940) and *12 Angry Men* (1957). He won an Academy Award for his role in *On Golden Pond* (1981). Fonda was born in Grand Island.

Joyce Hall (1891–1982) founded the Hallmark greeting card company. He was born in David City.

Malcolm X (1925–1965) was a civil rights leader. He was born Malcolm Little in Omaha.

Dorothy McGuire (1918–2001) was an actress. Her movies include *A Tree Grows in Brooklyn* (1945) and *Friendly Persuasion* (1956). McGuire was born in Omaha.

J. Sterling Morton (1832–1902) was secretary of agriculture under President Grover Cleveland (1893–1897). He founded Arbor Day in 1872 to encourage tree planting. Morton was born in New York and settled in Nebraska City.

Red Cloud (1822–1909) was an Oglala Sioux leader. He defeated the U.S. Army in many battles. Red Cloud was born at Blue Creek in what is now Garden County.

Standing Bear (1829–1908) was a Ponca chief who fought for Native Americans' rights to their land. He was born on a Ponca reservation in northeastern Nebraska.

Want to Know More?

At the Library

Bunting, Eve, and Greg Shed (illustrator). *Dandelions*. San Diego, Calif.: Harcourt Brace, 1995.

Gray, Dianne. *Holding Up the Earth*. Boston: Houghton Mifflin, 2000.

Levinson, Nancy Smiler, and Stacey Schuett (illustrator). *Prairie Friends*. New York: HarperCollins, 2003.

Nichols, John. *Big Red!: The Nebraska Cornhuskers Story*. Mankato, Minn.: Creative Education, 1999.

Porter, A. P. *Nebraska*. Minneapolis: Lerner, 2003.

Weatherly, Myra. *Nebraska*. Danbury, Conn.: Children's Press, 2003.

Welsbacher, Anne. *Nebraska*. Edina, Minn.: Abdo & Daughters, 1998.

On the Web

State of Nebraska
http://www.state.ne.us
To learn about Nebraska's history, government, economy, and places of interest

Genuine Nebraska: America's Frontier
http://www.visitnebraska.org
To find out about Nebraska's events, activities, and sights

Through the Mail

Nebraska Division of Travel and Tourism
P.O. Box 98907
Lincoln, NE 68509
For information on travel and interesting sights in Nebraska

Nebraska State Historical Society
P.O. Box 82554
1500 R Street
Lincoln, NE 68501
For information on Nebraska's history and historic sites

On the Road

Nebraska State Capitol
15th and K Streets
Lincoln, NE 68509
402/471-0448
To visit Nebraska's state capitol

Index

About the Author

Ann Heinrichs grew up in Fort Smith, Arkansas, and lives in Chicago. She is the author of more than one hundred books for children and young adults on Asian, African, and U.S. history and culture. Ann has also written numerous newspaper, magazine, and encyclopedia articles. She is an award-winning martial artist, specializing in t'ai chi empty-hand and sword forms.

Ann has traveled widely throughout the United States, Africa, Asia, and the Middle East. In exploring each state for this series, she rediscovered the people, history, and resources that make this a great land, as well as the concerns we share with people around the world.